The Three Spiritual Keys

Your only directive is to stay open to love

Katye Anna SoulWorks

Katye Anna Teacher of Soul

Published by: Katye Anna Soul Works Spring Grove PA
ISBN-13: 978-1973883395

Dedication:

I dedicate The Three Spiritual Keys to Anna, my soul, angels and God. I am humbled by the information that I have been given to share with those who read my books. My heart overflows with gratitude for my family, friends and students. Kathy and Lloyd, you have blessed my life since the day you were born. Kathryn Mummert, thank you for giving birth to me and being my mom. You and daddy taught me about the power of love. A special thank you, to Sally, Steve, Terry, Sara, Shirl and Antoinette. You have each supported me, loved me and held space for me in special ways. I am also grateful for the love and support I continue to receive from those who have birthed into spirit especially my dad, sister Debbie, Allan Sethius, and Johnny.

THE THREE SPIRITUAL KEYS
FOR EMPOWERED SOULFUL LIVING

Key One:
CONVERGE WITH OTHERS IN LOVE.

Key Two:
TAKE RESPONSIBILITY FOR YOUR THOUGHTS AND EMOTIONS.

Key Three:
WE CAN ONLY SUCCEED TOGETHER.

Katye Anna
TEACHER OF SOUL

www.KatyeAnna.com

iv

Together we can change the world, but first we must each become the change that we each seek to experience in the world.

As a teacher of soul, I seek to help each person who reads my words embrace the creative force of love that is within them.

I seek to help you stay open to love. I seek to help you remember the truth of your being and why your soul created a life on earth. I share a steady stream of consciousness with a group of 976 souls known to me as Anna, therefore when I write I use the words, I and we simultaneously.

Anna seeks to help liberate those of us in human from unconsciousness.

They do this by offering spiritual teachings such as the Three Spiritual Keys. The Three Spiritual Keys are offered by Anna to teach us about personal responsibility and what and how we create our experiences here on earth.

The Three Spiritual Keys are not new. Spiritual teachers have been teaching the path of love for eons. We will continue to teach the path of love until humankind remembers the truth of who they are and why they are experiencing life on Mother Earth.

As a teacher of soul, I use the term "spiritual key" as that which unlocks the doorway to spiritual dimensions and teachings of light which have been blocked off by unconsciousness. There is no veil blocking us from the world of spirit. For the spirit dwells within each one of us as well as around us.

The Three Spiritual Keys is a mindfulness pathway and becomes a way of life when used daily. Mindfulness is simply living in the moment.

Daily use of The Three Spiritual Keys will empower your life so that you will be the creative force of love you were born to be.

Daily use of The Three Spiritual Keys will help you stay open to love.

Daily use of The Three Spiritual Keys will give you entrance to a way of living, of being in the world, one that is in alignment with love.

Daily use of The Three Spiritual Keys will slowly activate deep inner knowing within you. This deep inner knowing comes from your soul and the world of spirit. The use of the Three Spiritual Keys unlocks your inner guidance system which connects you to the wisdom and guidance from your soul and the world of spirit.

Daily use of The Three Spiritual Keys will lead you onto a pathway of consciously creating your experiences in love. Conscious Creators use right speech to motivate, encourage and inspire other to action. They live from the heart and are guided by soul.

Our words and teachings are constructed to bring forth the creative expression of your soul which longs to express itself via your life. I seek to inspire all who read my words to be uplifted and imprinted with the remembrance of who you are, an incarnated soul living on earth for soul growth and soul expansion.

I ask you to take your time in reading The Three Spiritual Keys. At the end of each chapter you will find questions as well as key pillars of the soul. Take your time in answering the questions. Slowly begin to integrate into your life the Three Spiritual Keys for Empowered Soulful Living and above all enjoy the journey you call your life because it is one of your creation.

Blessings, Katye Anna

Chapter 1

Spiritual Key One:

Converge With Others In Love

,

THE FIRST SPIRITUAL KEY is clear, if an experience isn't in alignment with love do not be pulled into it. Do not give energy to that which is out of alignment with love. This requires conscious thought and action on your part. Of course, this is much easier said than done. As children, we were not taught that we are incarnated souls. Nor were we taught that we are each the creative force in our lives.

When we begin to awaken to the truth that we have the power within us to create all our experiences in love, I believe we will return to the beings of love we were created to be.

Pillar of Light

Your soul seeks to express itself as love via a physical embodiment.

Your individual responsibility is to ground more of soul into your physical body, thus you ground more soul into your life and onto Mother Earth. To be grounded means to be connected, and rooted into Mother Earth.

Grounding more soul into the physical opens pathways to soul guidance as well as a remembrance of the way of love.

When I was given the Three Spiritual Keys by Anna, I did not fully understand how much of our lives have been based on reacting to events, people and experiences that are not in alignment with love. We live in a world that continues to be created by Reactive Creating instead of Conscious Creating.

Reactive Creators, are always reacting to what someone else has created. Reactive Creators hold onto the past, refusing to let go. They get pulled into the drama, and shadow experiences and are usually called to action by rage, fear and anger. Reactive Creators use anger and fear to call others into action. They do not take responsibility for their thoughts and emotions, nor do they take responsibility for the energy they bring into the world. They live in the box of "I" and have little or no understanding of the connectiveness of all life.

As an incarnated soul, you were born to be a Conscious Creator.

Pillar of Light:

A Conscious Creator seeks to create in love and seeks to create experiences where the common good of all is at the forefront of what's being created.

This common good for all embraces the third spiritual key which is we can only succeed together.

Conscious Creators are moved into action by love. They are motivated to create change in the world that will impact the masses understanding that we can only succeed together. A Conscious Creator doesn't wait until an event or experience forces them to change, they take inspired action because they have observed the signs and understand how to move through life experiences with ease and grace.

A Conscious Creator understands that righteous indignation is not to be followed by conflict of any kind, thus uses the second spiritual key which is taking responsibility for your thoughts and your emotions.

Conscious Creators use right speech to motivate, encourage, support, uplift and inspire others to action. They live from the heart and are guided by their soul.

Many people who are Reactive Creators are often motivated by righteous indignation, but because they do not take responsibility for their emotions they quickly get lost in the wave of emotions which are chemically based. They charge into a situation using anger and fear which keeps the body-mind locked into an energy loop of flight or fight experiences. This is how homo sapiens have created experiences on earth for eons, in Reactive Creating.

The Three Spiritual Keys offers a pathway of mindfulness, conscious awareness of the moment, to get out of this energy loop of creating and recreating the same fear and anger based experiences.

A simple law of the universe is, whatever you give your energy to will increase. If you give your energy to something that is out of alignment with love you are now a part of the problem, not the solution.

Pillar of Light:

Righteous Indignation is a sign from soul that an experience is out of alignment with love.

People charge into an experience they believe is out of alignment with love, thinking and wanting to change it. Many times, they do this because righteous indignation alerts them that something is out of alignment with love. Righteous indignation is a sign from spirit, however, if you go charging into the energy which is out of alignment with love you will simply be fueling the experience you seek to change.

A conscious co-creator understands how to take the information from soul that something is out of alignment and create an experience in new energy.

Pillar of Light:

You cannot change anything in the energy it was created in.

By getting pulled into the "shadow experience" the righteous indignation which was a sign from soul now gets overshadowed by waves of emotions such as anger, rage and many times fear.

These emotions by themselves are just alerting you that something is out of alignment with love, however, when you sit in the energy of anger, fear and rage they fester and you begin to react to the experiences instead of consciously and creatively responding to it.

This brings us to Key Two, which is taking responsibility for the energy you bring into a situation. What started out as righteous indignation has now triggered a conflict reaction which does not allow anyone to converge in love. Some part of your being feels threatened emotionally, spiritually and or physically and the chemical dance begins setting off a conflict reaction within your body-mind. The body-mind does not know the anger of 2017 is different than the anger of 1822. The body-mind does not know that the fear of 2017 is different than the fear created in 1205 by a real impending death. Although the body is chemically based you are more than your body.

You are a spiritual being. You are an incarnated soul and you have both a physical and spiritual anatomy.

This conflict reaction is chemically based and chemically charged by the fight or flight impulse of the root chakra. A chakra is a part of your spiritual anatomy.

According to Anodea Judith, author of **_Wheels of Life: A User's Guide to the Chakra System_** "A chakra is a center of organization that receives, assimilates, and expresses life force energy. "Chakra" is a Sanskrit word meaning "wheels of light". When you begin to take responsibility for your thoughts and your emotions you will begin to change your chemical reactions, thus truly becoming the empowered being of love you were created to be.

As incarnated souls, you are both physical and spiritual, unfortunately you have not been taught that you are the creative force in your life. Nor have you been taught that you have the power of the universe to assist you in creating your experiences through love. Using the Three Spiritual Keys will change your chemical responses over time and create new responses within the body-mind. To do this you must take responsibility for your thoughts and emotions. We will discuss how to do this in greater detail in chapter two.

For now, begin to understand that you cannot create the change you seek by being pulled into the energy that is not in alignment with love. Being pulled into any experience that is not in alignment with love is counterproductive.

Key one is clear, converge with others in love and you cannot do this if you are in reactive mode.

The power behind this spiritual key is simple. If it's not in alignment with love don't give your energy to it. Move away from the experience. To move away from an experience that is not in alignment with love, you must stay open to love. When righteous indignation alerts you

that something is out of alignment you move
your energy away from the experience.

There can be no conflict without your help.

As you read our words you may be aware
that there is a voice within you, telling you that
you are only one person. This is true; however,
the creation of a forest begins with one seed.
Be the seed of love you were created to be.

Pillar of Light:

Your only directive is to stay open to love.

Fear and love, hate and peace cannot abide
in the same time-space continuum. There will
be many experiences where fear will try and be
your guide. Your job, your responsibility, is to
move your consciousness to a place of love.
Many of you are saying this is impossible. No, it
isn't, but it takes your full participation and
conscious awareness which means to be
mindful and to be present in the eternal present
moment. As soon as you are aware that an
experience is not in alignment with love, you
must move your energy and your thoughts
away from it. If you do not you will be
swallowed up by the experience.

You were created to be a conscious creator. You are a powerful and creative force of and for love. Your body-mind wants to remember this truth. When you begin to understand, and harness the creative force of love which is within you, you will begin to shift your consciousness at will and that which isn't in alignment with love will not be able to enter into your world.

Pillar of Light:

NOTHING comes into your experiences that you have not made an agreement to allow IN be it on a soul level or a personality level.

When you were a child, you agreed to what was real, and what was true. You agreed that the sun was yellow and the sky was blue. You made agreements what was good and bad, beautiful and ugly, you even made agreements as to what love looked like. You agreed to certain beliefs that were accepted by your tribe. Between the ages of birth to around six years old you created a vibrational signature. Your vibrational signature begins to send this information out to others via your energy field, which is a part of your spiritual anatomy. Your vibrational signature continues to change and expand the consciousness of you, however the core beliefs you agreed to between birth and six years old remain the same during your entire life unless you consciously release them and create new beliefs.

A belief will create your reality, thus your experiences, until someone or something comes along to change it.

Many of your old, outdated beliefs have triggers attached to them. If you didn't have the button you would not be triggered. I remind you the buttons pushed by others are not about them. These triggers are emotional and are fueled by a release of chemicals within the body, thus the trigger gets an automatic reaction from you. These triggers when pushed, will set off a rush of emotions. Your thoughts and emotions are translated into chemical expressions which send out information via many systems which include the endocrine glands. Your chakras and your endocrine system work together. This is all done automatically, this is why many times you aren't aware you have been triggered. You aren't aware that you are in Reactive Mode. A trigger always takes you into a conflict reaction. When you are in conflict reaction you are ungrounded, meaning you are not connected to your inner guidance system.

Your inner guidance system is your intuition. Your intuition is the voice of your soul. Your soul seeks to create experiences of love.

Your responsibility is to be conscious/mindful and when you have been triggered YOU must take command of your thoughts and your emotions. Even though the reaction feels automatic and is chemically based it is a choice to allow the reactive creating to continue.

I remind you NOTHING can be changed in the energy it was created. When you are triggered your emotional reaction will lead you into releasing that which is not in alignment with love because you are in conflict reaction. When you are triggered the only action, you want to take is taking command over your thoughts and emotions. Use your energy to bring yourself back into alignment with love. A triggered state will send you into a flight or fight response to a perceived threat of some-kind. When you are in a triggered state this is NOT a time to talk, and share your truth. When you are with someone who is triggered, this is NOT a teaching moment.

This is a time to take divine action which means to return to a state of love. As soon as you are aware that you are in an experience that isn't in alignment with love begin the process of moving out of the experience.

Here are a few simple steps to take.

1. As soon as you realized you are in a triggered state, thus a reactive state, begin to move your energy away from the experience. You do this by focusing on your breathing. Take a few deep breaths and remind your body-mind that you are safe. Using the breath in this way will help your body relax and stop the influx of chemicals from the fight or flight loop of the adrenal glands.

2. Simply putting your hand on your solar plexus chakra area and saying to yourself, I am safe can also help bring you back to the moment. This will begin to ground you. When you are grounded you are anchored in your body and anchored to Mother Earth.

3. The key is to move yourself away from the experience and or person/people that is not in alignment with love. Going for a walk, if you can, will help. Excusing yourself and

going to the bathroom will move you away from the energy.

4.   Once you are out of the energy/situation you can begin to move your body-mind back into love.

We remind you again that this spiritual key is clear if an experience isn't in alignment with love do NOT give it energy.

In Chapter Two we will teach you the Catch and Release Process that will lead you into a life of creating your experiences in love. Before you move on to Chapter Two take some time to answer the focus questions and to look over the key pillars of light from this chapter. As you begin answering the focus questions begin to think of yourself as a Conscious Creator.

Focus Questions:

1.   Write about one life experience that you changed by moving away from the experience that was out of alignment with love.

2. What old, outdated beliefs pull you into reactive creating?
3. Write about a current day experience that continues to push your buttons.
4. What kind of messages is your vibrational signature, sending out? (Hint you will know this through what kind of experiences you are having)
5. Write about an experience that you charged into wanting to change it, but ended up being pulled into the situation and/or experience.
6. *Pillar of Light:* "NOTHING comes into your experiences that you have not made an agreement to allow IN be it on a soul level or a personality level." Do you agree with this statement? Are you aware of any "agreements" you want to change? If so, what are they? Are you aware of an agreement that you have changed and in doing so changed created a new experience of love.

Chapter One Key Pillars of Light

Your soul seeks to express itself as love via a physical embodiment.

A Conscious Creator seeks to create in love and seeks to create experiences where the common good of all is at the forefront of what's being created.

Righteous Indignation is a sign from soul that an experience is out of alignment with love.

Your only directive is to stay open to love.

NOTHING comes into your experiences that you have not made an agreement to allow IN be it on a soul level or a personality level.

Chapter 2
Spiritual Key Two

Take Responsibility For Your Thoughts and Your Emotions

SPIRITUAL KEY TWO is clear, we are each responsible for the energy we bring into our experiences thus the energy we bring onto Mother Earth. Eons ago incarnated souls understood that this is a planet where experiences are created by one's thoughts and fueled by one's emotions.   This spiritual key unlocks teachings, that when implemented in your life, will set you onto a path where you begin to understand how to create a life of flow and one that is in alignment with love. A life of flow is creative and expansive and aligned with the dreams and visions of your soul.

Pillar of Light:

You were not created to live in a box.

Most people have no idea they are even in a box much less that the box is one of their creations. Every experience has been created by someone's thoughts. There are thousands upon thousands of experiences floating around on Mother Earth. Most of these experiences never enter into the very small box you call your life. You learned in chapter one that nothing comes into your life that you have not given permission to do so.

This is because you are the creative force in your life.

That said, what you allow into your box, thus your life, is based on what you agreed to before the age of six. Limits were imposed upon you as to what and how you created your experiences. These limits were based on what you were taught by your tribe, teachers and peers. They may have meant well and may not have known they were limiting you because they were simply teaching you what they believed was true, but they limited you nonetheless.

You were never taught that the thoughts you focus on create your experiences. Take a few minutes and think about this statement, "your thoughts create your experiences." Change your thoughts and you change your experiences. Taking control of your thoughts also means to align your thoughts with teachings of love.

Pillar of Light:

Every day is a brand-new day and is one of your creations.

This Pillar of Light reminds you that every day is a brand-new day. It is not a continuation of yesterday. Fear, anger, despair, heartache, joy, peace, health, etc. can only enter this new day if you allow them to do so. Using Key One, converging in love, begins with how you show up in your own life. You have the power within you to change direction. When you change your thoughts about an experience you will change your life.

When you realize, you have created something within your life that in not in alignment with love, you must move your energy out of the experience as we discussed in chapter one.

When you stop giving energy to that which is not in alignment with love the experience will fade away into the ethers. Love is the fabric, the glue and the container. People can only show up in your life in the ways that you can allow them to. This is true for the world at large. Your beliefs about a group of people or an individual will directly affect what kind of experiences you will invite inside your box, thus your life.

Today is a brand-new day and today what is true and what has always been true, is that you are the creative force in your life. You can rise above the circumstances of your life, but it will take your full conscious participation to do so.

One of the greatest detriments in seeking change within one's life is complacency. People are complacent and settle for what they have or don't seek change because they don't know where the new path will take them.

The smallest first step toward changing your life can set you onto a path of liberation and freedom. You and you alone must take that first step. No-one can take it for you.

You must begin where you are. Acknowledge what you have created and thank it for what you have learned from the experience. Now set that experience free. Next make a commitment to be the conscious creative force of love you were born to be.

Pillar of Light:

The path before you cannot be illuminated until you take a step onto it.

Your soul and the world of spirit are always nudging you to flow through the experiences of your life. The path doesn't light up like a Christmas tree, but it is there nonetheless.

Recently I met a man. I knew that we would have a good connection. A friend asked me if I thought he was "the one." I told her he could be, but I didn't know for sure. A few days later we spent the day together and really opened up to each other. The connection was a very powerful one. Two days later

I woke up knowing we had stepped onto a new path, one which could lead to a beautiful relationship.

The point here is the path had not been illuminated until we both stepped onto it.

I know it's a big step, but you will discover that when you decide to fully step into being the creative force of love you were born to be your life will change and along with it the world.

You might have heard the saying that you must become the change you seek to experience in the world, what you may not have heard is that when you become the change that you seek to experience in the world you create a stream of energy for others to build their own life of love, peace and joy on. As you change yourself, you become a catalyst of change for others. Truth is you are already doing this. You are always creating be it in the shadow or the light, be it as a reactive creator or a conscious creator.

As you begin to ground more of your soul into your physical body, you will begin to radiate this light to others.

Pillar of Light:

You have the power to choose a new direction for your life any time you choose to do so.

Changing direction for your life will not happen without action on your part. Affirmations and wishful thinking will not be able to break through the subconscious programing and old, outdated beliefs that have been the foundation of the life you are currently living.

Choosing a new direction must be followed up by action which must be followed up by more action.

Begin by affirming: I am the creative force in my life, and I choose to create a life that is in alignment with love. Remember, just affirming that you choose to create a life aligned with love is not going to change your life. By affirming something you are making a declaration of intention which begins to alert your subconscious mind and the universe of your intentions. That said, it is the subconscious mind which holds onto the limiting beliefs, this is why affirmations alone will not change your life.

At the end of this chapter you will be asked to write down a few areas of your life where you want to change direction. Take a few minutes and think about your life. Own it, own what you have created. Honor every lesson that has taught you something about love and then begin to use the tools offered in this book to help you create your life as the conscious creator you were born to be. Begin to think about the old, outdated beliefs you continue to create your life with. You might be tempted to jump to the end of this chapter and begin working with the focus questions, but continue reading because we have information that will help you.

Pillar of Light:

Every experience has something to teach you about love.

This is one of the most difficult lessons for people to embrace. As a teacher of soul, I have been asked many times how can there be a lesson about love in experiences such as war, rape, hate crimes, cancer, child abuse etc. Your souls seek to create experiences of love here on earth. That said, for eons personalities have learned many of their lessons the hard way. We have created shadow experiences on earth where the light seems to be blocked out. Many people believe you cannot know the light without the darkness. This has created learning your lessons via polarities. Love is in every experience, for love is the only thing that is real. As we have already said, when you stop giving energy to that which is not in alignment with love the experiences will fade away into the ethers.

Nothing can exist or enter into your box of experiences that you have not allowed to do so. When you allow yourself to enter into and stay in a state of love, you will begin to see your experiences through this place of love.

We understand that what we are saying will create conflict within your body-mind because your body-mind will quickly affirm all of the many experiences which have been created by reactive creating. Your body-mind will insist that the man lurking in the shadows intends to do you harm and that the many conflicts of war and hatred cannot be stopped by love alone. We remind you that everything in your world is a creation of thought. You have forgotten that everything in your world is energy. You see everything as a solid physical form, therefore when you seek to change something you are hindered by seeing it as solid. You cannot go through the physical wall because you see it as a solid wall, but when you realize that the wall itself is energy in motion you will learn how to break it down energetically. This is true with the many conflicts within your world.

There is only love, therefore nothing else is real and therefore it cannot exist without your help. When you hold onto experiences which are not in alignment you freeze the experience and yourself within this time space continue. When you change your thoughts about an experience you change the experience itself. Again, we remind you that it is not the experience that creates the wounding, it is your attachment to it. There is a message of love in every experience. This of course can only be seen once you have moved away from the experience.

When you change a belief, you change how you learn your life lessons. The choice is yours. Do you want to learn your lessons the hard way, in the shadow or the easy way in the light? Many years ago, I decided that I would learn my lessons the easy way. This choice opened my life up to moving through experiences with more ease and grace. Through the power of choice, I continue to learn my life lessons through love. I remind you just because a life lesson feels difficult, it does not mean it's not grounded in love.

As an incarnated soul, you were born to be creative, joyful, imaginative and resourceful. Because no one ever told you that you were born to be creative, joyful, imaginative and resourceful you learned to allow others to be the creative force in your life. For the most part, you have lived your life on autopilot, meaning unconscious and not mindful about what it is you are creating.

Today is a brand-new day. Today begin to see yourself and the world around you as an opportunity for you to create a life that is in alignment with love.

Pillar of Light:

It is not the experience that creates the wounding but your attachment to the experience.

I have seen major shifts in my students' lives when they begin to understand this spiritual key. It is NOT the experience which creates the wounding, and eats away at your heart, but your attachment to the wounding. By attaching to the experience that is out of alignment with love you begin to create a story and from that story you build other experiences. You have heard that victims are not born, they are created, this is true for bullies, rapist, terrorist etc. Something happened in their lives or the lives of someone in the tribe and a story was built around it. If you tell a story long enough, it will materialize on the physical plane. This is one core way old, outdated beliefs are created.

Change your story and you will change your experiences. To change your story, and your limiting beliefs begin to practice what we call *Catch and Release.*

Catch and Release is a spiritual tool to help you begin to release the old, outdated beliefs that take you into experiences that are not in alignment with love. When you become aware that you have been pulled into an experience that is not in alignment with love begin the Catch and Release Process.

To Catch and Release you follow a few simple but very specific steps.

Step One: In Chapter One you learned that as soon as you realize you have been triggered or have been pulled into an experience that is not in alignment with love, you must move out of the energy, thus the experience. Spiritual Key Two teaches you to take responsibility for your thoughts and your emotions.

Begin taking a few deep breaths. The breaths will begin to help your body/mind relax. Remember, when you have been triggered or are in an experience that is not in alignment with love, fear has kicked in. This means that your body/mind moves into survival mode. Fight or flight kicks in and your body is put on hyper alert. Your HPA axis kicks in and your body is flooded with hormones meant to help you survive the "attack". This perceived attack could have simply been someone you love disapproving of something they felt you could have done differently. You are triggered and your body goes into response mode.

By catching and connecting with your breath you will begin to alert your body/mind that you are safe. As you use your breath to ground yourself you can also tell your body/mind the current date and that you are safe. Simply say, it is July 17th 2017 (fill in the current date) and I am safe.

If you are with someone when an old outdated belief comes up and you have been triggered the next step you must take is moving out of the energy, thus the experience. This simply means excusing yourself and going to the bathroom, going for walk, or do whatever you can in the moment, to move yourself out of the energy, so you can begin the process of catching and releasing.

Once you have moved out of the energy you can catch whatever has been triggered by the old outdated belief or experience. This will usually take a few minutes. Ask for help from your spirit guides. It can be as simple as saying I've been triggered by (fill in the blank) and I need help to understand what the old outdated belief is.

Remember, you have thousands of old, outdated beliefs stored in the subconscious mind so it may take you a few moments to CATCH which ones are coming out of the shadows to be transformed.

When you do not take command over your thoughts and emotions you will be pulled into the experience, down the rabbit hole, and into the fire. Nothing gets transformed by being pulled into an experience that is not in alignment with love. NOTHING.

As a teacher of soul, I work with the angelic realm. Archangel Michael is the illuminator of sight. When we see clearly, we understand that there is

NOTHING to fear. I suggest you call upon Archangel Michael when you are ready to release the old outdated belief.

When you have a clear understanding of what you need to release you simply affirm, that this old outdated belief, person, and/or experience, has no power over me. I release it here and now, Michael here it is, I give it to you to transform. Be as clear as you can be about what you are releasing.

When you begin to take command over your thoughts and your emotions you will begin to understand the power behind the words, "*you are the creative force in your life.*" We remind you that when you have been triggered this is not a teaching moment. By this we mean this is not a time to talk. Silence is your friend when you are in a triggered state.

In the beginning of the "Catch and Release" process your vibrational signature is not strong enough to hold the new vibrational signal and this is why affirmations help once you catch and release the old outdated belief and patterns. An affirmation is a statement of empowerment. The gift of catch and release is one day you realize that you no longer get your button pushed by a certain person and/or experience. This is how you know that the old outdated belief has been released.

This is how you change your vibrational signature and your life.

Remember, every day is a brand-new day. Every day you have the opportunity to show up in your life knowing that you have the spark of God within. You are expanding the very consciousness of God.

Today, as a Conscious Creator you must begin the process of clearing out beliefs that are not in alignment with love. This takes your full participation in your life. Today is a new day and you and you alone can move away from the current circumstances of your life. One way of doing this is implementing the Three Spiritual Keys into your daily life.

Focus Questions:

1. List several areas of your life where you are living in a box.
2. Write about two areas of your life you want to change. What old outdated beliefs and patterns keep you in the experiences? What action must you take to move out of the situation and/or experiences?

3. Where in your life are you complacent?
4. List 3 experiences you continue to be attached to, even though the experience happened years ago. What is the story you continue to tell yourself about the experience? Are you ready to let go of your attachment to the experience?
5. Write about a shadow experience that taught you about love.

Chapter Two Pillars of Light

You were not created to live in a box.

Every day is a brand-new day and is one of your creation.

The path before you cannot be illuminated until you take a step onto it.

You have the power to choose a new direction for your life any time you choose to do so.

Every experience has something to teach you about love.

It is not the experience that creates the wounding but your attachment to the experience.

Chapter 3

Spiritual Key Three

We Can Only Succeed Together

SPIRITUAL KEY THREE is clear, we need each other to succeed. It has been eons since personalities had this spiritual truth at the forefront as they created experiences. In Chapter one you learned the difference between being a Conscious Creator and a Reactive Creator. A Conscious Creator seeks to create in love and seeks to create experiences where the common good of all is at the forefront of what's being created. A Conscious Creator understands that in order to succeed together everyone must each take responsibility for the energy they each bring into the world because everything you do will be experienced on some level by everyone else on the planet. To succeed together, each person must think about what they are creating at any given moment and how it will affect the collective experiences on earth.

Pillar of Light:

There is no "I" on any plane of consciousness except on earth.

Knowing that the key to succeed is unity, your soul, gathered together in the hall of records and made core soul agreements with other souls. Souls understand that earth is the ONLY plane of consciousness within God, where one experiences separation. Each soul understands that although they each have their own individual life plan they need many other souls to help bring it into fruition on the earth planes of consciousness. Every soul creates a life plan understanding that its life plan will create life experiences for the collective masses.

Seeing oneself as separate is an illusion one must break through to begin to understand this third spiritual key. Because you are energy beings, you meet each other via your soul connections long before you meet each other on earth in the physical.

When you break free from the illusion of the "I" you will begin to see the connectiveness of all life.

Pillar of Light:

A core soul agreement is I will be that which you have asked me to be so that you can be that which you need to be. May we seek to do this on earth in love.

In the first two chapters, you learned that nothing happens in your life that you have not invited into it via a soul agreement and/or an agreement you made when you were a child. We also taught you that it is not the experiences which create your wounding it's your attachment to the experiences.

Keeping these two pillars in mind, we would now like you to begin to understand that everything you have experienced is for soul growth and soul expansion. Every soul seeks to create an incarnation on earth where it will help to shift the experiences into experiences of love. Your soul created your life with the knowing that everything you create on earth will leave an energy imprint long after you have returned to spirit. The implications of this, when fully understood and integrated into your lives is powerful. For your soul's plan to succeed you, the incarnated soul, must wake up from the hypnotic trance you have been under for most of your life.

To succeed together you must begin creating as Conscious Creators. This means that you must each have in the forefront of your minds that what you create in any given moment must be in alignment with love and must be for the common good of all. This means everything you do, every choice you make, every thought you give your energy to must add to the collective consciousness of love. We realize as you read our words you may be feeling that this is a daunting task, but if you truly seek to heal the wounds of those living on mother earth this is one pathway to do so.

You must live and create with the common good for all at the forefront of everything you do.

This means do nothing until you ask yourself, is the experience I'm creating in alignment with love. Once you begin to understand how powerful you are as the creative force within your life you will begin to imprint new experiences of love.

If the experiences you are creating or participating in aren't in alignment with love, they cannot be for the common good of all therefore you must not give your energy to it.

Today begin to consciously create your experiences, asking yourself what experience will this create for others? Begin where you are, by this we mean look at the life you have created and begin to make changes within your own life that will have the possibility to create an experience that will help everyone involved move into a resonance of love.

You continue to hold onto old patterns of living and creating because you have grown complacent. You were not taught that you are part of the collective whole, nor were you taught that you are the creative force in your life. Today begin to take full responsibility for the world you have created. Do not blame others for the circumstances of your life, but take full responsibility for your life, for you and only have allowed the experiences into your box.

We now call on our friend Archangel Michael to illuminate your sight so that you can begin to see what you have created. In the future call upon Archangel Michael to help you see clearly and to GENTLY remove the bags from your head.

Be gentle with yourself as you begin to remove the bags over your head. You will be surprised how many ways and how many experiences you participate in everyday that are not in alignment with love and do not take in consideration the common good of all. As the bags covering your sight are removed, we ask you to be gentle with yourself. Honor the past and move away from it, by doing so you begin to remove its power over your life. We remind you that the experiences of your life are not what creates your wounding, it's your attachment to the experiences and the stories you tell yourself.

As you begin the process of embracing being a Conscious Creator we have another suggestion to make, allow others to have their experiences they need to have while at the same time not getting pulled into them. Most of your experiences have been created by someone else. Many of your experiences you created from a state of unconsciousness as well as from limiting beliefs you agreed to when you were a child.

Today is a brand-new day. Create this day in love.

Pillar of Light:

Allow others to have the experiences they need to have.

Everyone has had an experience where you are having a wonderful day. You feel great and aligned with love. You receive a phone call, a text, email, read something, heard something on the news or someone said something that is not in alignment with love. Suddenly, before you know it you are being pulled into the drama, the situation and/or the experience. Before you know it, you are now feeling agitated, and the energy of you begins to change.

We believe it is important for you to understand the energy of you as well as how you move in and out of your experiences.

As a child, you were not taught about the energy of you. You have not been taught that when someone or an experience is not in alignment with love you shift your energy to meet the other person and/or experience so you can enter into it. This is another form of reactive creating. Instead of allowing the person to have his or her experience you allow yourself to be pulled into it, and in doing so you change your vibration of peace you had been feeling for one that allows you to enter into the other person's experience. You were never taught that when you enter into an experience that someone else has created you literally have shifted your energy to meet them where they are at.

This meeting others where they are energetically, occurs even before you meet someone in the physical. It also occurs through random occurrences when you are simply out in a public place. I remind you that to enter someone's experience you have to be an energetic match. This is wonderful when the experience is in love and you both merge through fields of love, but think how often you move into someone else's experience and shift from a place of peace and love to one that is agitated and/or fearful and angry.

As a conscious creator, it's your responsibility to begin holding an energy field of love. When you allow the other person to have the experience they need to have this frees you to continue creating your day, and your life in love. As you begin to understand and live in the power of creating your life in alignment with love, you will begin to be the change you seek to experience in the world.

Pillar of Light:

A world of peace, joy and love already exist within the time space continuum within God.

At the beginning of this book I wrote, "I believe, at our core, we each share the same dream. We dream of living in a world where there is "enough" for everyone to live lives of freedom, peace and love. I believe deep within each one of us, we share a dream of living in a world where no one is starving and where war and hatred are memories of an ancient past."

We have shared that nothing comes into your world without you agreeing to allow it in. To experience something in this time space continuum within God you must be willing to allow it into your box of experiences. Nothing can enter into your life without your willingness to allow it in, this is true of the plight of others. Nor can change of ANYKIND enter into your life unless you are open and willing to allow the change to occur.

Change of any kind can only occur if you are willing to see the experiences which need to be transformed. This is true collectively as well as individually. Complacency keeps you from seeing the plight of others. Your bags over your head filter out the experiences of others because you continue to see yourself separate from your brothers and sisters who share this planet with you.

The plight of other people, nations, ethnic groups, and the world at large are not even on your radar because you have not allowed these experiences inside of your box.

Collectedly you have created a world of duality where the collective belief is that to experience light you must experience darkness, to experience love, you must know hate and sorrow, to experience power you must experience powerlessness.

Collectedly you have created a world of have and have nots.

You continue to create a world of duality.

Your only directive is to stay open to love. Love is kind. Love is patient. Love is tolerant. Love is. We say to you again and again your only directive is to stay open to love.

The key to staying open to love is loving yourself.

You will find that love is kindness you must first give to yourself and then to others. Love is patience you give first to yourself and then others. Love is tolerance you give to yourself and then to others. Truly, we say you cannot give these soul qualities to others if you have not opened your own heart to them.

A world of freedom, peace and love already exist within God. One by one you are finding the keys that will unlock the doors to this world, but even with the keys you and you alone must decide if you want to enter once the door is open. To enter you must be willing to cast aside the old, outdated beliefs which have led you into a world of have and have nots. You must begin to ask yourself who you must become to enter this place of peace, love and freedom. If you do not hold the vibration of peace, love and freedom within you, you will not be able to stay in the time space continuum within God where peace, love and freedom exist.

Throughout this book we have encouraged each one of you to embrace the magnificence of who you are. We believe we have offered you tools and perhaps helped you begin to embrace how amazing you are. When you begin creating with the common good for all in the forefront of everything you do you will begin the slow process of turning the earth planes of consciousness back to a place of love. We believe converging in love, taking responsibility for the energy you bring onto the planet and embracing that you can only succeed together as a human race will be one huge step forward for those of you who are living on earth.

Be gentle with yourselves as you seek to move back into a resonance of love and remember your only directive is to stay open to love.

Focus Questions:

1. When you look at your life can you see experiences that you are currently giving your energy to that are NOT in alignment with love? List a few

2. Looking at the list you created choose one or two and ask yourself what steps you must take to bring the experience into alignment with love? Sometimes bringing something into alignment requires a huge shift while others will require that you simply refuse not to participate in an experience that isn't in alignment.

3. Are there certain people and/or experiences that you have trouble allowing them to have the experiences they need to have? If so list them and list the hook if you can. (the hook is why you get pulled into something that isn't in alignment with love)

4. Do you believe we can create the change that is required to shift the earth planes of consciousness from a world of duality, a world of have and have nots? If so what is a belief you must change to be a part of this GREAT shift of consciousness?

5. The key to staying open to love is loving yourself. Do you give yourself doses of kindness, patience and do you love yourself?
6. List several old outdated beliefs and patterns you are now aware of that you weren't before reading The Three Spiritual Keys.
7. What are one of two big takeaways you have from reading this book?

Chapter Three Pillars of Light

There is no "I" on any plane of consciousness except on earth.

Allow others to have the experiences they need to have.

A core soul agreement is I will be that which you have asked me to be so that you can be that which you need to be. May we seek to do this on earth in love.

A world of peace, joy and love already exist within the time space continuum within God.

Chapter 4

Spirit of Divine Collaboration

Message from Anna

Greetings,

WE ARE ANNA. We are a group of 976 souls who seek to work with those of you who are in human form. We offer teachings that when used will transform your life and your consciousness to one of love. We share a steady stream of consciousness with Katye. Katye is an Awakener. The codes of light were activated during several stages of her life. Through activations and energy transfers Katye's spiritual DNA was activated. She is a homospiritus. This simply means Katye is able to hold more light within her physical body and her energy field. This is how it is possible for Katye to share a steady stream of consciousness with a group our 976 souls.

We have given you The Three Spiritual Keys as a pathway of taking personal responsibility for that which you create on earth. Souls understand what personalities have forgotten which is the importance of Divine Collaboration on EVERY plane of consciousness within God. Of course, collaboration of any kind without cooperation cannot occur on any plane of consciousness. Souls understand that without cooperation from many other souls even the most thought out and agreed upon soul plan will not be successful on the earth planes of consciousness.

This is true for those of your living on earth, you cannot succeed without one another. To succeed, together you must move into and embody the spirit of Divine Collaboration.

While every soul seeks to liberate its life plan on earth they understand that there is one core soul agreement which all others are built upon, it is, "I will be that which you have asked me to be so that you can be that which you need to be. May we seek to do this on earth in love."

Every soul seeks to create experiences of love.

The only directive you are given is to stay open to love. Our teachings, including The Three Spiritual Keys are built upon returning the inhabitants of earth to the way of love.

The earth planes of consciousness is entering another cycle where great shifts of consciousness will be experienced by the masses. These shifts in consciousness will require those in human form to come together in love. Divine collaboration and the spirit of cooperation among every tribe of the nation as well as the world of spirit will bring about the peace many seek to experience on earth.

Many will experience these shifts of consciousness in great fear, this is another reason we have given you The Three Spiritual Keys. Love and fear cannot abide within the same time space continuum of God. Daily use of the Three Spiritual Keys will help to ground your experiences in love and begin to activate the codes of light contained within your spiritual DNA.

The codes of light, when activated within you, will make it IMPOSSIBLE for you to stay in the hypnotic trance where you experience yourself as separate from the whole. As your codes of light are activated, you will see with illuminated sight. You will begin to see the many experiences on earth that are not in alignment with love. Compliancy will be an experience of the past and the people of earth will become Conscious Creators.

When the codes of light are activated, you will begin to remember the truth of who you are.

You are an infinite being of love.

In the year of 2012 the earth planes of consciousness experienced a SHIFT. This SHIFT was not immediately experienced or sensed by the masses. That said, there were many who experienced the SHIFT as an opening, and an expansion of self as well as the entire universe. Many have called these people the dreamers, some have called them the misfits and crazies.

We call them the awakeners because they have activated within themselves the codes of light that will help others to wake up from the hypnotic trance inhabitants of earth have been under for eons. The codes of light are universal.

Awakeners seek to change the world through love, for they understand that love is the only directive. Awakeners embrace a multidimensional approach to life. Awakeners see themselves and everything within God as waves of energy in motion. Awakeners are not fixated on the experiences of the outer world, but understand that the outer world experiences are created for soul growth and soul expansion. Awakeners do not seek fame, glory or fortune, although many have found that these are often experienced when one's life is in alignment with love. Awakeners are Conscious Creators and seek to create that which is for the common good of all sentient beings.

When we speak of Divine Collaboration we speak of the world of spirit and those of you in human form working together to restore what many refer to as heaven on earth. When we speak of Divine Collaboration we also speak of all sentient beings, *which of course includes the animal, plant and the mineral kingdoms.*

Daily use of the Three Spiritual Keys will bring your life into alignment with love and will activate the codes of light. Living a life which includes compassion and mercy for all will also activate one's codes of light. The codes of light are contained within your spiritual DNA. We understand in the era in which you are currently experiencing consciousness little is known about your spiritual DNA.

When the codes of light are activated, you will experience an awakening within your life. For many this awakening will occur over time for a few of you this awakening will happen very quickly. As your codes of light are activated, you will begin to experience discontentment in areas of your life that are out of alignment with love. You may experience being uncomfortable in your own skin. Be loving with yourself as you begin to shift your life into one that is in alignment with love.

Everyday seek to create experiences of love. Use The Three Spiritual Keys to guide you through the experiences of your life. Take care of your physical body. Your body is the vehicle for the expression of your soul to shine through.

When your light codes are fully activated, you will walk as one with the Creative Force of the universe. Connection to a higher level of wisdom and guidance will be your new norm. As you listen and integrate this wisdom and guidance into your life you will begin creating your experiences in love.

As the codes of light are activated, you will begin to communicate through the language of light. Light language breaks through the words that humans use to communicate. Light language is a universal language and releases an angelic vibration of love in the energy field, hearts and minds of all who experience it. While words can be used to communicate, words also create a divide.

Within the language of light there are rays of every color encoded with information, sacred geometry as well as ancient wisdom. You have already experienced light language during your dreamtime. This language is universe meaning those of you in human form, as well as those of us in non-physical form speak the language of light.

As you move into this new way of being, of living, we suggest that you pay attention to the signs of spirit that are all around you. Begin listening to and following the direction you receive from spirit. Begin using the great resources of the universe as you use the Three Spiritual Keys to transform your life. Through the spirit of Divine Collaboration and cooperation use The Three Spiritual Keys to begin creating experiences on earth where the common good of all is at the forefront of what is being created.

Take time every day to laugh and to enjoy the gift of life you have been given.

Every day walk in gratitude. As you move through your day remember to connect with spirit and be mindful of that which you are creating.

Be diligent in the use of The Three Spiritual Keys.

Converge in love, take responsibility for your thoughts and your emotions and know that we can only succeed together. Be courageous and forthright as you move into being a Conscious Creator and know that you have the entire universe cheering you on.

We thank you for this opportunity to speak to you. We hold you in the light.

We are Anna

Key Pillars of Light

Chapter One:

Your soul seeks to express itself as love via a physical embodiment.

A Conscious Creator seeks to create in love and seeks to create experiences where the common good of all is at the forefront of what's being created.

Righteous Indignation is a sign from soul that an experience is out of alignment with love.

Your only directive is to stay open to love.

NOTHING comes into your experiences that you have not made an agreement to allow INTO your life.

Chapter Two

You were not created to live in a box.

Every day is a brand-new day and is one of your creation.

The path before you cannot be illuminated until you take a step onto it.

You have the power to choose a new direction for your life any time you choose to do so.

Every experience has something to teach you about love.

It is not the experience that creates the wounding but your attachment to the experience.

Chapter Three

There is no "I" on any plane of consciousness except on earth.

Allow others to have the experiences they need to have.

A core soul agreement is I will be that which
you have asked me to be so that you can be
that which you need to be. May we seek to
do this on earth in love.

A world of peace, joy and love already exist
within the time space continuum within God.

About the Author

Katye Anna: For over twenty years, Katye Anna has been sharing her gifts and messages of transformation and empowered soulful living. Katye Anna is a teacher of soul, transformational author, speaker, and retreat facilitator. Katye Anna embraces life as a mystical, magical, and spiritual journey; one she chooses to consciously walk with God.

Gifted with the ability to travel the many planes of consciousness within God, Katye Anna walks between worlds. Katye Anna has a direct connection to the world of soul and the world of spirit. Communicating with the world of spirit is as natural as breathing for Katye Anna.

Katye Anna writes and teaches from her heart and is guided by her soul, Anna, and spirit teachers. Her gifts of travel and sight allow her to do what many authors and spiritual teaches can't do - give firsthand descriptions of the many planes of consciousness within God.

When she writes about the tunnel of light, she writes from her firsthand accounts of helping people more into the light. When she writes about her sister Debbie's cabin in heaven, she can describe it in detail because she spends time with her there. When Katye Anna describes the Hall of Records where souls gather together to finalize soul agreements, she is describing it as she has seen it during her travels. Katye Anna uses her connection with the world of spirit to share the teachings of Anna. In 2013, Katye became the voice for Anna (thus the name Katye Anna). Anna is a group of 976 souls who no longer experience consciousness on earth. Anna teaches from the higher planes of consciousness and seeks to bring forth teachings that will help personalities take responsibility for the energy they bring to earth and their experiences.

The insight from Anna is endless. Katye Anna's books, classes and retreats offer teachings and guidance meant to help shift people's awareness about being incarnated souls.

Further, her work illustrates how our experiences here on earth are just a small part of the journey of the soul. Katye Anna provides teachings and experiences to help clients and students release old outdated beliefs and patterns. Once that is accomplished, they are able to lead empowered lives fueled by one's soul and the universe.

Together with Anna, Katye teaches students and clients how to consciously connect with their own soul.

Katye Anna believes everyone has a direct line to the world of spirit. Through meditations and spiritual guidance, Katye Anna opens those she works with to embrace their own unique line of communication with the world of spirit. With her messages of love, she seeks to show that everyone can live an empowered life.

Information

For information about Katye Anna's ongoing classes and retreats go to: www.KatyeAnna.com

To contact Katye Anna for speaking engagements, write to: Katye@katyeanna.com

Want to sign up for a Mind Mastery Class go to: katyeanna. com/mind

To find out more information about Katye Anna's Next Life Mastery Year Long Program go to: katyeanna.com/life

Join Katye Anna on Facebook at:

https://www.facebook.com/KatyeAnna

Made in the USA
Middletown, DE
10 July 2021